JOURNEY TO PEACE

JOURNEY TO PEACE

MY LIFE OF ADVENTURE, DESPAIR, AND COMING TO FAITH

Mary Riem

JOURNEY TO PEACE
MY LIFE OF ADVENTURE, DESPAIR, AND COMING TO FAITH

iUniverse books may be ordered through booksellers or by contacting:

iUniverse
1663 Liberty Drive
Bloomington, IN 47403
www.iuniverse.com
1-800-Authors (1-800-288-4677)

ISBN: 978-1-4917-5495-5 (sc)
ISBN: 978-1-4917-5494-8 (e)

Library of Congress Control Number: 2014921878

Printed in the United States of America.

iUniverse rev. date: 01/13/2015

DEDICATION

To my parents, Virgil and Esther Sharratt, who exemplified what it is to live life to the fullest and be devoted to God. Their love, nurturing and prayers were invaluable to me.

Acknowledgments

Father God, for his saving grace love, guidance, wisdom and protection.

Jon and Pat Sween, for their spiritual counsel and vision for my profession of faith.

Marcia Hadfield, for her mentoring, prayers, friendship and encouragement to write this book.

Theresa Gomes, for her faithfulness as a true friend over the years, for her encouragement in my Christian journey and her assistance with this book.

Friends and Family, for helping me be a better person, for being there for me when I struggle and for joyfully participating in life's adventure with me.

All of those over the years who were used by God to inspire, instruct and encourage me. I am so thankful that he brought you into my life.

INTRODUCTION

My home overlooks the fairways of a golf course. As I view the beauty I am filled with awe that I am privileged to live in such a serene setting. This scene is a mirror of my inner being, I am at peace.

I find it remarkable that the serenity I have is constant despite changing situations. Circumstances ruled my emotions for much of my life. I had a restlessness that caused me to constantly seek new experiences to provide enjoyment and satisfaction. Contentment evaded me despite having close relationships, experiencing job success, traveling extensively and participating in exhilarating sports.

I know now that what I was missing was spiritual grounding. For many years I was an agnostic and cynical about religious beliefs. During a time of profound emotional and physical distress I had what I would term my first God sighting. Since that time I have had numerous 'sightings' that have led me to a strong faith. My life has been filled with both global travel and travel of my soul. Many times the two have been intertwined. I will be sharing with you the story of my life and highlight some of these journeys. In doing so I must divulge the 'skeletons in my closet' that frankly will surprise many who know me.

It is my desire that this book will not only engage and inspire you, but will prompt you to choose the peace of God.

CONTENTS

CHAPTER 1

THRIVING IN MY FORMATIVE YEARS

Just outside the city limits of Seattle sits an acre of land where my parents built a home and developed a farm. I was the oldest of four girls and was fortunate to be in a loving and cheerful environment. The days were filled with constant activity. There were many chores which vied for school work and recreation time. Each one in the family had a role in managing all that needed to be done. The animals needed to be fed, the barns stocked and cleaned and the garden planted, weeded and harvested. Each of our four goats needed milking twice a day. It was not uncommon for one goat to produce two quarts of milk a day. Mom did most of the milking but I sometimes helped. We always had an abundance of milk and gave the surplus to friends.

My sisters and I had specific farm projects to help us learn how to manage a money-making endeavor. Colleen, who was a little more than a year younger than me, fed the chickens and sold eggs. Joan, the sister younger than Colleen, raised rabbits which were sold for pets or used for meat. It seemed to me that she had the easiest job because the rabbits were always producing more! My youngest sister, Shirley was ten years my junior, so didn't have a project until after I had moved from home. She eventually specialized in training and showing horses. I enjoyed raising purebred Samoyed dogs to sell. My dog named Sonya had eight to ten pups at least once a year. I made enough money to buy a horse and pay for its keep.

Medical care of the animals fascinated me. Veterinarians visited our farm from time to time. My mother was taught how to administer some of the needed care, such as giving injections and treating wounds. Seeing the healing effects of treatments sparked in me the desire to learn about medical care. I was thrilled to reap the rewards of my learning by saving the life of a newborn pup with mouth to mouth resuscitation. This incident prompted me to choose to become a nurse when older. In high school I became involved with the nursing association, studied Latin and learned a little community health nursing from a public health nurse in my neighborhood. She allowed me to accompany her on home visits to learn some nursing skills.

In addition to nursing, I was fond of cooking. My mother taught me how to cook with the fresh produce from our farm. My earliest accomplishment was making a cherry pie at the age of six. I'll never forget the time I worked for hours to make an elaborate four course meal as a gift to my father for his birthday. When he began eating the mixed salad at the beginning of the meal he discovered a slug inside the lettuce. That event ruined the meal that I thought would be so special.

Meat such as chicken, rabbit, goat and pork also came from our farm. My least favorite cooking chore was plucking the chicken feathers after the butchered chicken had been immersed in boiling water. It was a smelly and messy task. In the summer we had freshly harvested fruits and vegetables. Mom canned a lot of them for winter enjoyment. I never fully appreciated at the time how fortunate I was to have all the varieties of good food.

Outdoor activities and sports have always appealed to me. My family often enjoyed hiking, camping, swimming and boating. In the winter we went sledding and downhill skiing. Mom had learned to ski in Upper Michigan and passed her knowledge on to us. Dad loved to fish and scuba dive. I learned to dive with him but didn't do it often because I had difficulty managing the heavy and cumbersome equipment. I never became much of a fisherman either. I think my dad was hoping that I would be a good salmon fishing partner. He patiently and painstakingly taught me how to use the reel, hook the bait and cast it out. I'll never forget the shock on his face when I once accidentally threw both the rod and reel overboard when attempting to cast the bait!

Hiking and camping in the mountains was one of my favorite activities. I enjoyed seeing the beautiful country and viewing a variety of wildlife. Cooking at camp was often memorable because my parents would catch trout for grilling. Sometimes for special trips we would bring the horses to the mountains for an extended stay. We'd load them up with camping gear and food and take them to a base camp destination. From there we could trail ride at leisure.

I became quite accomplished at horseback riding and loved to ride in a local field near my home. The field had a plentitude of open space that would enable me to let my horse run at full speed for a long distance. My horse was fast and riding was exhilarating. Some days I'd ride a few miles to reach a local beach along Puget Sound. I have fond memories of riding the sandy shore and taking my horse for a swim.

Summer vacations sometime included cross- country travel by car or train to Michigan to visit my maternal grandparents. The adventure of travel was exciting to me. I loved seeing unfamiliar territory and meeting a variety of people. These experiences planted in me the seed of desire to one day explore more of the United States and foreign countries.

Descriptions of my younger years would not be complete without mentioning church involvement. My family attended a local Baptist church every Sunday morning and evening. Sometimes we also participated in a prayer meeting on Wednesday night. Our minister was an impassioned speaker and I enjoyed his preaching. I embraced the teachings and even entertained the idea of working as a missionary in a foreign country. Music was a memorable part of the church service. I enjoyed singing songs with the congregation which were led by musicians. Most often there was a pianist, organist and violin player. Several members of the church were accomplished musicians who performed solos. The impact of the music inspired me to learn to play an instrument. The accordion became my instrument of choice.

The church had a youth program which I enjoyed. It was packed with a variety of activity. In addition to learning about the Bible, there were sports, social events, summer camp and crafts. My mother often taught crafts for summer vacation Bible school, which was attended by more than one hundred youth. She was an expert in leather tooling and using the leather to make bags and belts. She also did painting and creative work with copper.

Her involvement and commitment to the youth program was such that she once rode her horse in a parade with banners announcing the youth activities. My father was also involved with the youth and especially enjoyed teaching children ages three to five years old. He was gifted in telling stories and being comical. Quite often he would make animal figures out of balloons to give each child. They loved him like a father.

Now that I have an adult perspective I can truly appreciate what a remarkable childhood I had. I will always be grateful for such extraordinary parents who exposed me to so much learning and fun. They were excellent role models of how to live life to the fullest.

It saddens me now to know that I caused them a great deal of heartache when I had a crisis of faith in my early adult years and renounced my childhood beliefs. Little did I know that as I pursued my goals of independence and adventure, I would drift from my childhood experience of joy and security into a place of discontentment and, at times, pain.

CHAPTER 2

RESPONSIBILITIES AND ROMANCE

At seventeen years of age I graduated from high school. After investigating nursing schools I chose to apply to a local community college to obtain an Associate of Arts degree in nursing. There were two reasons for this choice; I had limited financial resources and within two years it would be possible to become a Registered Nurse. I reasoned that I could begin a nursing career and then in the following years obtain a higher education when I had more money and had a better idea of what specialized training interested me. I was fortunate to be immediately accepted into the community college nursing program despite tough competition.

I lived at home with my family while attending college. The days were long and difficult. I often had hospital practice in the mornings and classes in the afternoons and evenings. My fascination with the sciences and medical practice kept me motivated to endure the work. Finally I finished my studies and passed the RN boards to become a certified nurse at the age of nineteen. I was exhilarated with the prospect of beginning a career and living independently.

I chose to obtain general nursing experience in a large Seattle hospital affiliated with the University of Washington. My role was to work as a staff nurse on a thirty bed medical-surgical ward. I was responsible for overseeing the care of one half of the ward, which involved supervising two Licensed Practical Nurses in the care of the patients and administering all of the medications. The work was overwhelming at times but satisfying, interesting and educational.

Soon after beginning my career I moved from my parent's home to an apartment that I shared with two nursing students who were coworkers. Their encouragement and emotional support was invaluable. We became such close companions that I don't recall ever having a major disagreement. My first adventure as an adult was having my roommates join me on a trip to Canada.

An added bonus to my new living situation was that my apartment was located near the fraternities for the University of Washington. I had been dating a young man since high school who attended one of them. We were anticipating marriage when he completed his studies. I wanted to live in close proximity to him and see him often. I soon discovered that he had a change of heart about his commitment because of wanting to experience the single lifestyle for several more years. We broke off our relationship at one of his fraternity parties. My sadness was somewhat quelled by the consolation given by one of his friends whom I had known from my childhood church. It was an unusual twist of fate that his friend had been my first romantic crush in middle school. Little did I know then how much this surprise encounter would affect my future.

Within a few weeks we were seeing each other regularly but not exclusively. After two months passed we found that our desire was to have a serious relationship. We had many interests in common and I was strongly attracted to his caring and energetic nature. Not much more time passed before I had fallen in love with him and accepted his marriage proposal. Although we were young, age wasn't something we thought would be a problem. We both managed many responsibilities. He had been working and attending school for three years and I was a full- time working professional. We made a decision that after marriage we would spend quality time together as a couple, including extended travel, before buying a home and beginning a family.

CHAPTER 3

ELATION AND TURMOIL

A large church wedding was held after a brief engagement. My husband was twenty- one years of age and I was nineteen. Our families were delighted that we were together because they felt we were so well suited for one another. I viewed our marriage as being one that would always be strong because we loved each other so much. I'll never forget my elation as we left the wedding celebration under a hail of rice to begin our lives as a couple.

My spouse and I had very little time together during the first few months of marriage. I was working full time and he was attending classes at the University of Washington to finish his degree in business. The romance of living together was far from my idealistic expectation. I consoled myself with the thought that our situation would improve when he graduated from school. I soon found out that I was mistaken.

When he obtained his college degree, he was unable to get employment due to Seattle's economic recession. We moved to another city for him to begin a career as an accountant. The only job available to me in our new locale was night shift. I wasn't able to sleep well during the day and my work environment was extremely stressful. This resulted in me feeling constantly tired and emotionally drained. To add to the stress, my husband didn't like his job. Within six months we decided to move back to Seattle. I easily obtained work at a local hospital but my husband wasn't hired for many months after that.

After we settled into a new apartment and had more stability and enjoyment in our lives, my husband announced that he wanted to buy a home and begin a family. He also mentioned a desire to have me stop work in the future to be a stay at home mom as his mother had done. I was bewildered and upset that he had changed his mind on our pre- marriage agreement. My unwillingness to support his ideas caused friction in our relationship. His way of coping was to buy an elaborate sound system and listen to music. I coped by working more and socializing. I was anxious and began to feel trapped in a relationship that did not foster my dreams of an ongoing career and travel.

Stress began to take its toll on me. My weight was steadily dropping from a lack of appetite. I assumed the cause was my anxiety. Unfortunately that wasn't the only reason. A sudden high fever and shortness of breath resulted in my admission to the hospital where I was diagnosed with tuberculosis. One of my lungs collapsed due to an infectious fluid collection. After a long hospitalization I returned home to recover. My mother graciously cared for me each day while my husband was at work. It took a month for me to be independent with daily routines. Gradually my strength increased and I gained endurance through walking and bike riding. During this time my husband was attentive and our relationship improved. We enjoyed our evenings together and with friends. I returned to work after about a six month absence.

Within a few months of my return to health, the issue of starting a family surfaced. My husband wanted to buy a home and have a child. The farthest thing from my mind was to develop firm family roots and take on a financial debt.

My dream and strong desire was to have adventurous vacations together before we began a family. We were at an impasse. As time passed I discovered he wasn't willing to compromise on the issue. Once again our relationship became strained and I was unhappy.

Friendships became my solace and I spent a lot of time socializing. The philosophy of those around me began to erode the confidence I had in the religious views I had embraced in my youth. They considered it unreasonable for any religious belief system to claim to be superior to another in its views about God or anything of the spiritual nature. Their bias was that the Biblical teachings of absolute right and wrong were not reasonable for modern day society. The prevailing viewpoint was that something was wrong only if it caused harm. My inclination was to embrace this idea because it was a simple guide for life and not guilt- provoking.

Eventually, I concluded that I had in effect been 'brain washed' into believing in God and the Biblical teachings. It had been the only philosophy I had known and I reasoned that if there were so many other world views that the Christian claim of ultimate truth was suspect. I conceded that there may be a spiritual world but did not think it could be known in a concrete way. My new belief system became a humanistic one of faith in my ability to determine my destiny. My goal would be to live life to the fullest and strive not to cause harm to another. I began having a secret affair but reasoned that it was acceptable as long as it didn't hurt my husband.

Sadly though he eventually found out and was deeply hurt. I regret that to this day. We separated and later sought out a counselor to help us reconcile. This was no avail because I yearned for a different lifestyle and was unwilling to compromise. The decision was made to obtain a divorce. We had only been married for three years.

A huge rift developed between my parents and me because of my not choosing to honor my marriage commitment and my rejection of Christianity. They were deeply saddened that I had turned away from a faith in God. Whenever I had contact with them they verbalized their disapproval and vehemently urged me to change. To avoid this conflict we became estranged from each other. I also did not continue contact with my sisters because they were not in support of my decisions.

CHAPTER 4

ACHIEVEMENTS AND OBSESSIONS

The years following my divorce were focused on developing work expertise, having fun activities and creating a financial base that would allow me to explore the world. I was tempted to take the little money I had saved and begin immediate travel but decided to wait.

A major reason that I was not in a rush to travel was that I enjoyed my living situation. I had rented the lower level of a beach house that had floor to ceiling windows in the front. The front yard was level with the bulkhead, so when the tide was high the Puget Sound water was eye level with my living room and bedroom. The living room was especially inviting because of a fireplace and natural wood paneling. It was a perfect place to have respite from the stress of work and to entertain friends. Despite full time work I was able to enjoy recreation in the evenings and during days off. Running the trail along the beach near my home became a near daily routine. Life was going exceptionally well, which seemed to confirm that I had made good choices.

The hospital where I worked was opening an Intensive Care Unit for medicine and surgery patients. Previously there had only been a Cardiac Intensive Care Unit. The idea of working with complex critically ill patients in a unit setting appealed to me. I hired into the unit and began working with experienced nurses to learn their skills and attended classes to learn what was required to be competent in this specialty. The training was fascinating and at the same time quite intimidating. Eventually, I gained the skills and knowledge to have the confidence and ability to participate as one of the ICU team. We worked well together and each of us gained a sense of fulfillment and pride in seeing the positive effects of our work. Many of my coworkers became good friends and have remained so despite passing years.

The work in the Trauma ICU continued for many years until I decided to pursue a Bachelors degree. I was confident that the expense and effort would pay off with the dividends of more knowledge, a sense of accomplishment and possibly a career advancement.

Seattle Pacific University accepted me into their Bachelor of Science nursing program. While attending school I continued part time work at the hospital. The grueling schedule ended after two years when I graduated with my degree.

Not long after graduation I was rewarded with a promotion to a leadership role at work. My responsibilities were to coordinate National Institute of Health funded research within the Burn and Trauma critical care units. This work was a unique opportunity to help improve the care of critically ill patients. My job satisfaction skyrocketed.

A personal motto became 'work hard and play hard.' Time off work was spent participating in sports and socializing. I joined an athletic club and became friends with a number of hard core athletes. Their fitness inspired me to train for competitions. Within a few months I was competing in racquetball tournaments and working out every day. My fitness proved itself when I was able to climb Mt. Rainier with a team of doctors who were studying the effects of high altitude. Exercise became so enjoyable that I began to participate in 10 kilometer runs and eventually in triathlons.

The down side of becoming so sports- minded was that I became rigid with my food intake to maintain a low body fat for competition. Eventually my demanding exercise combined with restrictive eating took its toll. I began having times of excessively eating to satisfy my cravings for food and then would exercise vigorously in an attempt to burn off any excess calories. I didn't realize it at the time, but this pattern was the evidence of an eating disorder.

A man I had become seriously involved with enjoyed gourmet cooking and hosting dinner parties. I began to gain some weight as a consequence of my frequent indulgence in rich food. When I compared myself to other athletes I became self- conscious of my body and became preoccupied with dieting. I would have periods of severe food restriction and weight loss but then stop dieting and regain the weight. This cycle of behavior distressed me and lowered my self- esteem. My body image was severely distorted. I was actually a normal body weight, but compared to very thin athletes I viewed myself as fat.

A life- impacting event occurred at one of my boyfriend's dinner parties. Halfway into the evening I chanced to go to the bathroom and he was there vomiting. I expressed concern and he casually responded with the statement that he wasn't sick, but just getting rid of the food so he could feel better and be able to continue enjoying the party. In discussing the issue later with him he told me that he regularly "got rid of the food" if he ate and drank too much. He did this so that he would not gain weight or get a hangover. I had never heard of anyone doing that before but was intrigued with the idea, despite considering it repulsive. He was a smart and accomplished professional who considered it acceptable so I figured it might not be so bad for me to do on occasion. Its appeal to me was that I could prevent weight gain. What I was totally unaware of then is that this activity is termed bulimia and that it is not only a dangerous and unhealthy activity, but it usually prompts a vicious cycle of binging and purging.

An eating disorder can be an ugly beast that takes hold and keeps one in its grip. What began as occasional bulimia became regular daily purging within a few months. I had shame over this behavior, so did not tell anyone about my personal struggle. It seemed that the more I binged, the more food I craved and fantasized about eating. I sought a counselor to help me but had only limited periods of freedom from my bondage. I was referred to a physician who prescribed medication to help eliminate the cravings, but they had minimal effect.

Fortunately, my health wasn't dramatically affected and I was able to continue with my job and sports. I began to learn windsurfing as a fun distraction from my inward turmoil. Sadly though, my former vitality and happiness escaped me. My serious romance of several years came to an end and I began to revisit my plan for overseas travel.

It seemed that the time had come for me to realize my longstanding goal to explore the world. A dramatic change in life circumstances and environment was also something that I thought would help me resolve my eating disorder.

CHAPTER 5

ADDICTION AND ESCAPE

Funds to support extended travel would be provided by my retirement fund, which necessitated the termination of my job. With sadness, I said good-bye to my hospital 'family". A very different life was on the horizon for me.

For recreation during my time of transition, I initiated a membership at a local windsurfing club located on Lake Union in Seattle. The business had a retail store, spa facility, board storage and a floating dock to launch from. To defer membership costs I hired on as a part- time windsurfing instructor.The casual lifestyle without the stress of hospital work gave me a sense of freedom and a propensity to party. A few acquaintances introduced me to cocaine. I knew its dangers but rationalized that occasional use would be harmless. This idea was reinforced by my observation that my 'user' friends did not seem to be adversely affected by it.

To my delight, I found that this drug suppressed my appetite in addition to giving me a pleasant euphoria. This enticed me to use it more often. I fooled myself into thinking that I could use it moderately and not become addicted. Within a few weeks I craved it constantly, and found that I needed more and more to achieve the same effect. It affected my sleep and enjoyment of every activity. It also was depleting my nest egg of money. The reality of my addiction sobered me into action to remove myself from the source. I began to make plans for immediate travel. An around- the-world trip was not yet possible so I chose to go to Asia. The idea of going alone intimidated me so I sought out a friend to join me. We planned a three-week-trek in the mountains of Nepal with added excursions into Thailand and Hong Kong. Our trip began in early fall. We stopped in Bangkok, Thailand for a week on our way to Nepal. It was fun to explore the city sights, experience the exotic atmosphere and dine on the delicious spicy food.

Following our initiation into the Near East culture in Thailand, we boarded a flight to Nepal. The plane landed in the outskirts of Kathmandu, its capital city, and I was fascinated by its vibrant mix of culture and beauty. It had a dramatic juxtaposition of traditional culture and modern development. Shops, family tenements, offices and restaurants lined multiple narrow streets. Traffic was a free-for-all between cars, motorcycles, bicycles, rickshaws, animals and pedestrians. Open- air fruit and vegetable markets bustled with activity. Elaborate Hindu temples adorned with carvings and prayer flags were strategically located throughout the region.

Within a brief period of time, my friend and I settled into a pleasant travelers' lodge in Kathmandu. Jagged snow capped peaks and lush countryside could be seen from our hotel's outside terrace. We arranged to spend a few weeks in the city to sightsee and make final arrangements for the trek. There was a variety of excellent ethnic food available in Kathmandu. The meals were inexpensive and delicious. Unfortunately, all the good food was a difficult challenge for me because my appetite was not being suppressed by cocaine. Cravings for cocaine were frequent as well. In desperation I again resorted to a drug for relief. My choice was codeine. It could be purchased at local pharmacies without a prescription.

I bought a large supply to last me for several weeks. A small dose each day was enough to normalize my appetite. Once again I was free of the nagging cravings and could enjoy the travel to come. My travel partner was a dear friend and fellow nurse. She had greatly assisted in obtaining information about the mountain trek we desired to take. A close friend of hers was a physician, Dr. Bezruchka, who had written one of the primary guides for trekking in Nepal.

Our trek of choice was the Annapurna Circuit which circumnavigated the Annapurna peaks and traversed approximately 140 miles in and out of mountain valleys. Lush green rice paddies terraced the hillsides in the warm lower elevation, but high country was mountainous and cold. The majority of tourists that trek in Nepal pay to join an organized adventure travel group for convenience and safety. We desired to have a more private hiking experience, so we took a tent and basic cooking supplies. The tent provided privacy, a comfortable environment for sleep and a place to take a daily sponge bath. The cooking supplies were for our morning tea. We packed a variety of snacks but not ingredients for meals. The meals would be purchased from villagers along the way.

Two Nepalese brothers were hired from a trekking agency to help us carry gear and act as our interpreters with the villagers. They were friendly and helpful but spoke minimal English. The trekking experience became a dream come true. We enjoyed the varied beauty of the country and the congeniality of the locals along the way. Each day we hiked approximately eight hours through rugged terrain and then pitched our tent in the evening wherever we could find a good location. One time the only space to pitch the tent was on the flat roof of a small barn. The interaction with the Nepalese people was heartwarming and sometimes comical. Our porters would help us communicate with the villagers and negotiate a price for their sleeping place and the meals for all of us. Food was cooked over an open fire in the center of the two room home. Lentils and rice was typical Nepalese food every day. Occasionally, a meal had a little vegetable, an egg, dried yak meat, or local potatoes.

A frightening event during the trek occurred when crossing a 17,650 foot pass of snow. While camping in the village below, we were warned by the locals of high winds forecasted for the following afternoon which might render the crossing impassable. We decided that by leaving at daybreak we could get over the pass before the storm. Early the next morning we packed up camp to begin our climb. It was so cold that my water bottle had frozen inside the tent and the condensation on the tent walls had become ice. Our porters were ahead of us and carrying most of the gear. Halfway over the pass the conditions became so treacherous due to ice that, despite protests from our help, we turned around to go back down. We proceeded down the way we had come with our porters in the rear.

My friend and I were so preoccupied with negotiating the steep terrain that we were not aware that partway down our porters had defied our instructions and went for the pass with our gear. Our situation was daunting because we had no extra clothes for warmth and no sleeping gear. The reality was that we needed to get over the pass to find our porters as soon as possible. Luckily, we met a climbing party and were given their support in negotiating the treacherous icy slopes. The wind storm held off long enough for us to cross the high pass. Within a day we eventually caught up with our porters. They were remorseful but explained that they feared a long delay in getting back to their homes if we had waited for the storm to pass. Despite their apologies they were given a stern reprimand and to our relief, proved trustworthy during the remainder of the trip.

Warm autumn days graced our last week on the trail. Trees on the hillsides were aglow with red and yellow leaves. Clear blue skies offset the granite and snow of the nearby peaks. Villagers seemed more cheerful and welcoming than usual. Hiking seemed effortless and energizing. It was the perfect conclusion to an arduous but wonderful trip. The last night of the trek we pitched our tent in a cow pasture owned by a local farmer and celebrated the conclusion of the trip at the campsite. We were both ecstatic to have accomplished so much.

High in the Himalayas of Nepal

The return to the states proved to be unusually stressful. Acclimating to the western lifestyle was only part of the difficulty. My eating disorder reared its ugly head again because I no longer was suppressing my food cravings with a drug. My consolation was that I did not return to using cocaine.

CHAPTER 6

SAUDI ARABIA; THE CHALLENGES AND HEALING

I desired to continue a travel lifestyle but knew my remaining funds were not adequate. The idea of obtaining work overseas became intriguing because I would have the adventure of experiencing a foreign country and earn money at the same time. After careful research regarding the employment opportunities available, I decided to apply to work for the ARAMCO Company. (Arabian American Oil Company) This company had been established when the Americans assisted the Saudis in discovering and extracting oil. Several large communities were developed in the eastern region for the oil business workers and their families. In addition to housing there were recreational facilities, offices, a mosque, a grocery store and a large medical facility.

Much to my delight I was hired by ARAMCO to work as an ICU nurse in the company hospital for the community in Dhahran, near the Persian Gulf. A tedious process of supplying necessary paperwork resulted in a delay of several months before I could leave the States. A good friend provided a room in her home for me to rent while I patiently waited. An all consuming focus for me during this time was athletic activity to balance the effects of my eating disorder. I still kept this sickness a secret and hoped that healing would come when I went to Saudi Arabia. Finally my departure day arrived and I had a heartwarming send off at the airport.

Upon arrival in Dhahran I was met by a friendly American woman, who I discovered would be my nursing supervisor. My designated living area was a 500 square foot unit with a small private courtyard. It was located near the company's large golf course which was scenic but had no grass, just varying grades of sand. The Dhahran community of approximately 11,000 people was a mix of Saudis and expatriates. Over fifty different nationalities were employed by ARAMCO. The diverse ethnic mix was fascinating but nothing could have fully prepared me for the culture shock of living and working in Saudi Arabia.

I had received 'induction training' about the culture prior to my arrival, but adjusting to the atmosphere and cultural mores was much more difficult than I had anticipated. Saudi Arab men believed that women were to be subservient to them and that they were not entitled to equal rights. Arab women wore black *abayas* (full-length over covering) when outside the home. In stark contrast, the Arab men wore white *thobes* (cotton robe like tunic) with red and white checkered head scarves, called *gutras*. Travel for the women was to be with her husband and they were forbidden to drive cars. Fortunately for me, the non-Muslim women were not required to wear black and could drive a car on the company compound. All women within the ARAMCO community could travel without a man to specific outside locations on the company bus. This was not without its difficulties however, because of the frequent negative reaction of men to women. A humorous side note to this was a time when an owner of a store that I visited was very amorous towards me instead of disrespectful. He wanted me to marry him and said I was worth a lot, at least six camels!

The attitudes of the Arab men towards the female medical staff were generally favorable within the hospital because they appreciated the service that was being provided. Despite this, there were several times when disrespect prevailed. Once I was on the phone taking an important call about an incoming emergency and had the phone jerked out of my hand by a man who was visiting his mother and demanded that I stop what I was doing to get her a drink.

My job at the ARAMCO hospital was more difficult than any I had ever experienced. As charge nurse for ICU, I was responsible for overseeing the care of a wide variety of critical medical and surgical patients. The majority of the staff were non- westerners. It was not uncommon for me to work with six different nationalities in one day. Communication with the staff was difficult at times, but even more of a challenge was the fact that most of the patients spoke only the Arabic language. I had anticipated that many of the critically ill patients at the company hospital would be westerners but discovered that they rarely sought treatment in Saudi for life-threatening illnesses. Intensive Arabic studies became an added job necessity.

After having weeks of training in formal Arabic, I found what I had learned was of limited help because most of the patients spoke a folk Arabic dialect. One other aspect of work that was especially challenging was the work schedule. Patient care workers rotated to a different eight hour shift each week. Typically, this meant working seven shifts in a row with two days off prior to beginning the next series of shifts of days, evenings or nights. My sleep and wake schedule was continuously in a state of flux.

If it was not for the friendships and support of my co- workers I could not have coped with all the work stress. My supervisor became a close friend who I would socialize with on time off. She has continued to be a good friend.

Time away from work was refreshing. The ARAMCO bus provided service to a beach where a private 'yacht club' was located on the Persian Gulf about twenty miles east of Dhahran. Some employees had motorized boats and a few had windsurfing gear. Eventually I was able to purchase some windsurfing equipment and have a man register my 'boat' for me. It was such a treat to be part of the beach community and enjoy the windsurfing.

Dhahran beach for ARAMCO employees

The landscape was one of giant ski slope like sand dunes which abruptly ended at the turquoise blue water where palm trees dotted the shoreline.

Sand dune along the Persian Gulf shore

When not enjoying recreation at the beach I was able to relax at what I considered my oasis within the ARAMCO community. This was an extensive athletic facility with an attached outdoor swimming pool. The view from the pool was of palm trees and a colorful variety of blooming desert plants. The many hours I spent swimming in this beautiful environment have left indelible imprints on my memory.

I never tired of the dry and sunny weather. It was such a welcome change from the often rainy and cool Seattle climate. I didn't even mind the 120 degree days of summer with the humidity often at 90 percent, because I could be in air conditioning, at the swimming pool or cooling down at the beach. On rare occasions there would be bad weather with severe dust storms which obliterated daylight for hours. Contrary to the Saudis' dread of these harsh conditions, I found them exciting.

The social experience was the highlight of being an expatriate worker. Typical western entertainment such as theaters, music halls and bars were not available because of the Muslim culture. Consequently, friends would gather for dinner parties to socialize. Each one attending would provide food for a buffet sampling of ethnic dishes. These parties were fun but proved to be troublesome for me. The large varieties of enticing foods were difficult for me to resist and as a result, my eating disorder become more of a problem than it had been in the States. Self discipline would typically last for a just a short time before I'd over indulge and end up purging soon after. This was revolting to me but I wasn't able to break the habit. It was frightening to know that the negative physical effects of my eating disorder could be life threatening. I despaired of ever getting out of the pit I was in. It was laughable that at one time I was convinced that I would always be able to control my destiny. Just when I had lost all hope of relief from my torment, a series of events rocked my world.

My closest friend within the ARAMCO community confided in me that she had an eating disorder. She said she needed to tell someone and had decided to confide in me. She was interested in attending an Overeaters Anonymous group that existed for women living in the compound and wanted me to go with her for support. She had no idea that I needed the group more than her. I agreed to go with her under the pretense of wanting to be a supportive friend. I had a glimmer of hope that somehow it might help me, as well.

When we went to the meeting we were introduced to the twelve step program and heard stories from other women about their struggles with overeating. Part of the program was choosing a 'higher power' to be a primary support. For most, they identified a personal God as their source. My friend followed suit because she had a Christian faith. She embraced the program wholeheartedly that night. Soon after the meeting, I decided to be honest with my friend and divulge my secret. I felt a strong need to have support and knew she could be trusted to keep it confidential. It was a tremendous catharsis to tell her what I had been going through. She suggested that I pray for healing even though she knew I was a non- believer. When I dismissed her suggestion, she said that she would keep me in her prayers. I admired her faith and the integrity she had in living out her faith. We had had many discussions about why she believed what she did and I was impressed that she always had knowledgeable and compelling responses to my questions and cynicism.

Many days went by and I kept thinking about my girlfriend's suggestion to pray. My sickness was worsening and I was despondent. It was not uncommon for me to fall asleep in tears of despair. One night I was so miserable that I decided that saying a prayer was better than doing nothing. I figured I had exhausted all the possible treatments and might as well see if it would have any effect. I ended up praying that if there was a God that wanted to interact with me, that he show himself to me by making me well. I fell asleep that night not anticipating any result.

A sound sleep ensued and I felt totally refreshed when I awoke the following morning. I had a sense of well- being that had evaded me for years. Something else that was different in how I felt was that I didn't have my usual ravenous hunger. As the day progressed, I was surprised to discover that my food cravings were absent and that when I ate I did not desire to eat as much as usual. My thoughts revisited the prayer I had said the previous night, but I doubted that it could have been the cause of the physical changes I was experiencing. I surmised that good rest must have caused the temporary positive effects within me.

Much to my amazement, many weeks passed without a return of my eating disorder. This was the first time in several years that I was free of my food cravings without drugs, and I realized that it was not a coincidence that the dramatic change occurred after I prayed for healing.

I was confounded by the fact that despite my unbelief, God had revealed his reality to me and confirmed that He was not an impersonal force in the universe. I resolved to investigate a variety of belief systems through discussion with others and study, with the hope of determining my own convictions about God. This goal was daunting because of so many competing religious views.

I wrote a letter to my parents to explain my change of heart regarding the reality of God and informed them of my beginning inquiry of faith systems. This was a balm to their heart pain over my rejection of God and tremendously opened the channels of our communication.

The milieu of Saudi Arabia was not conducive to the study of other religions. The import of non- Muslim information was prohibited. Fortunately, an exception to this was that expatriates were allowed to have books and scriptures for personal use. At times I had the opportunity to read the material owned by those I came to know within the ARAMCO community. Each vacation from the Arabian continent offered me the opportunity to read all that I desired. I gradually gained a basic understanding of many religious beliefs, but after many months was still not sure of what I believed.

My spiritual search began to wane as I became preoccupied with finalizing my employment with ARAMCO and pursuing more world travel. Vacation travel while in the Middle East had taken me to numerous countries including Africa, India, Indonesia and Sri Lanka. Most of my trips had been solo and on a budget. The appeal of this mode of travel was that it was relatively inexpensive and I could experience cultures at a grassroots level. I traveled with a backpack, used local transport and stayed in small tourist lodges or family homes. I was as some might say, "bitten by the travel bug." The more I traveled, the more I desired to continue traveling.

Chapter 7

Adventure Travel

In August, after being employed for three years by the Saudi ARAMCO company, I gave my resignation. I had accepted a job with a British tour company to work with a team who facilitated hiking tours in the Alps. This opportunity had presented itself when I had been a client of the company while vacationing the previous year. I had become friends with the owners and trek leaders, one being a British man with whom I had an attraction. We had been corresponding since meeting and envisioned traveling together. Our goal was to explore more of Europe after our completion of employment in the fall. The company van would be ours to use for a month as compensation for driving it back to the company home base in London, England.

Working for the tour company was a fun challenge. The trip began in the valley of Chamonix, France and followed the 100 mile hiking route around Mt. Blanc, which involved passing through Switzerland and Italy. My job was to work with three other employees in guiding the hikes, preparing meals and setting up camp each night. The support van with all the camping gear would be shuttled each day to the hikers' new destination in a mountain valley. The tour for the clients proceeded exceptionally well and I confirmed during this time that my boyfriend and I were compatible travel partners.

The autumn colors were in all their splendor when my companion and I set out to see other parts of Europe. We gravitated to the mountains of Italy and France for a remarkable season of rock climbing, mountaineering and camping. During this time our relationship deepened and we entertained the idea of a future together. We did not want a long distance relationship, so we made plans for him to come to the States after our time in Europe. Soon after bringing the company van back to London, I left him in England to return to the States to reunite with family and friends. Later he would join me for more travel.

The winter had just begun when I arrived back home from overseas. The warm welcome that I received from my parents was in dramatic contrast to the chill in the air. I was invited to stay in their home and within a few short weeks we were enjoying quality time together. My sisters and I also reunited and soon were making up for lost time in our communication. Among many of the conversations with my family was what I had learned in my quest to establish a personal faith. They intently listened to me and were very supportive of my need go at my pace in this process.

The time at home with family and friends was very satisfying but did not change my desire for more travel. I purchased a Volkswagen camper van to drive to Baja, Mexico to spend the remaining winter and then explore the southwestern U.S. desert country the following spring. My boyfriend had a hiatus from working and would be able to join me. I found it remarkable that my parents displayed a great deal of grace by welcoming him when he arrived. They did not accept that he and I were together without being married, but were congenial despite their disapproval.

Travel proceeded according to plan with my partner to Baja and then later throughout the canyon lands of the western US. While exploring these scenic regions it seemed as if we were in a fairytale world. Each landscape had a uniquely captivating beauty.

Beach enjoyment in Baja, Mexico

The months passed quickly and when my boyfriend and I returned to Seattle we parted again to enable him to return to work in Europe. I settled temporarily in my parents' home and obtained work through a nursing registry agency which would place me in a variety of local hospitals in need of temporary help. This type of employment enabled me to work without committing to a contract. With this arrangement I forfeited employee benefits but could dictate my work schedule.

The summer months of being home and not traveling were more difficult than I had envisioned. The readjustment to a busy city pace and the demands of work after a year of absence was emotionally draining. The added stress of missing my boyfriend's companionship and not having the frequent emotional highs of adventure travel seemed almost more than I could bear. It was astounding to me that despite the stress, my eating disorder did not return. My food cravings were gone and I enjoyed eating without the desire to overeat. This reconfirmed to me that I had been healed.

When the fall season arrived I left Seattle to join my boyfriend for more overseas travel. This time we would be trekking for three weeks in the Himalayas of Nepal. Our desire was to see the Langtang region. He was to see the country for the first time and I had not yet visited this area of Nepal. The several weeks we spent together was extraordinary as we hiked in the mountains from village to village and obtained lodging in local families huts. We carried basic cooking and camping gear to use when necessary. Each day presented us with breathtaking views of peaks over 18,000 feet high. The congenial and interesting interaction with the Nepalese and other trekkers was very satisfying. At the end of this trip my boyfriend began to make connections to develop his own guide service for clients traveling in Nepal. He went back to London to develop his trekking business and I went home to Seattle.

CHAPTER 8

SOUL SEARCHING
AND DISCOVERY

When I returned home I was ready to have a slower pace for the winter. For the first time since leaving Saudi Arabia my attention returned to my spiritual quest. Soon I was reading many hours a day but the many conflicting religious claims to truth bewildered me. My consolation was that I knew I could trust God to answer my prayer for guidance and wisdom.

It readily became apparent that the best way for me to make an informed decision regarding what I believed was to carefully investigate the foundational basis of one belief system at a time. By doing so, I could gradually eliminate those which were not credible or congruent with reality. The tenants of the Christian faith were my first focus for two reasons. Firstly, I knew that the basis for Christianity was a faith in a personally interactive God. Secondly, I desired to articulate to my parents the reasons for not embracing their beliefs. My rejection of Christianity was primarily based on my bias that the teachings were unreasonable, based on the Bible, which was full of contradictions and myth. Christians claim that the Bible is without error and is a book written by men who were inspired by God's Spirit to write His revelation to mankind. I assumed that in a relatively short time I would easily identify specific reasons to dismiss the Christian faith.

This focus of inquiry was timely because a local protestant church had just begun regular meetings for people investigating Christianity. Many different topics were discussed and questions were encouraged. The meetings were lively and thought-provoking. During one of the meetings I connected with a man and his wife who assisted with the discussions. They offered to provide me with specific books related to my focus of inquiry and I readily accepted their generosity.

The first resources I investigated were related to determining the accuracy and reliability of the Bible. The vast historical and archeological verification of numerous Biblical accounts was impressive and indicated the writings were not mythical. The inconsistencies that I had expected to find were not present. The uniqueness of the Bible became very apparent. I found that it is like no other book in that it is actually a compellation of 66 books written over 1500 years by 40 different authors who lived on three different continents. The cohesiveness of the author's theme of God's love, interaction with man and provision for a relationship with Him, was especially striking. What got my attention even more than all of this was the fact that the Bible is the only book in the world which has over one hundred precise and specific prophecies which have come to pass exactly as predicted. When considering all of these findings I felt it was reasonable to accept that the Bible had a supernatural origin.

On a regular basis I would obtain more books from my new spiritual mentors and have coffee with them to address further questions. I wondered if the Bible writings had been altered over time as it was copied and translated into many languages. What I found was that it has more manuscript evidence to verify its accuracy in transcription than any other ancient document. There are some grammatical errors that have been made during the copying process but those errors do not alter the accuracy of the message. This information led me to accept that the Bible copy available today is trustworthy.

The next step in my investigation of the foundational Christian beliefs was to determine if there were convincing reasons to accept that Christ was God in the flesh and that he arose from the dead following his crucifixion. There was a vast amount of literature available on these two controversial topics. Careful evaluation of the information caused me to support both as true. It was humbling to discover how harshly I had judged Christianity without knowing much about it. My skepticism had led to the acknowledgment that God had answered my prayer to reveal His truth to me. An inner prompting kept nudging me to make a declaration of what I believed but I procrastinated in doing so.

I wasn't ready to identify myself as a Christian and commit to being a Christ follower. Quite frankly, this reluctance was for selfish reasons. I knew that many friends would judge my choice as foolishly embracing a worldview that they viewed as judgmental and naïve. Also, I was afraid of how my commitment would change my hedonistic lifestyle.

CHAPTER 9

TURKEY; ENCHANTING EXCURSIONS

An inner angst and restlessness prompted me to embark on another travel adventure. I desired to explore Turkey for several weeks. It was springtime so I knew there would be good weather and fewer tourists at the places of interest. Unfortunately, my boyfriend was unable to join me due to his business commitments. I arranged a layover in London to visit him for a few days. We had been communicating frequently and were patiently enduring the time apart. Something that bothered me a great deal was that he had expressed his concern about the effect my spiritual interest would have on our relationship. He was an agnostic who was critical of religion. I hoped he would eventually change his viewpoint as I shared with him what I had learned.

Elation would be the best description of my emotion upon reconnecting with the man who held the strings to my heart. This emotion dramatically changed within a few days because it became clear that we could not have a future together. There was more than one reason for this realization but a key factor was his firm stance on having nothing to do with spiritual matters. I left for Turkey with a heavy heart.

It was late afternoon when I arrived in Istanbul Turkey. The exotically beautiful city was mesmerizing. My pension room was located within view of the grand Palace built during the Ottoman Empire. The streets were alive with activity and music was spilling out from local cafes. My thoughts took me back to being in Saudi Arabia as I heard the distinctive rhythmic call to prayer from the local mosque. The emotional pain in my heart was soothed as I anticipated traveling by bus from city to city to visit places I dreamed of visiting.

Over the next six weeks my experiences did not disappoint me. Some that were especially memorable were; visiting idyllic beach towns where I enjoyed local food at quaint cafes on the waterfront, walking through many ancient cities that had remnants of amphitheaters and temples rivaling those of Greece, and scuba diving at ancient wreck sites to view preserved artifacts. I enjoyed traveling by sailboat to offshore islands to see old cities with historical military fortifications and staying in a remote villages where I observed farming and country life as it has been for centuries. All along the way I was blessed by interesting conversations with friendly locals and other foreigners.

A highly memorable and life-changing experience occurred in the Cappadocia region of Middle Eastern Turkey. This high plateau area has a fairy tale landscape due to the erosion of volcanic rock into shapes of whimsical cones, chimneys, mushrooms and pillars. These rock formations are large, some reaching as high as one hundred and fifty feet. Locals have hewn out homes and places of worship in the rock and have established farming in the valleys. The area is known as a historical refuge for people seeking hiding from threat of harm. Christians during the 4th century made underground cities here to escape persecution from the Romans. They formed complex tunneling living areas which were eight levels deep in some places. The volcanic rock would absorb the smoke from their fires so that they could live without being detected. In the 7th century the Christians living in this area created elaborately frescoed cave churches that have remained intact until now. My accommodation while visiting Cappadocia was in a room of a home carved out of the rock. I loved the unusual cave atmosphere but found the lack of heat uncomfortable.

Cappadocia landscape

Home hewn out of rock in Cappadocia

Joining a tour group to explore the many valleys of the region was not appealing to me because I wanted a peaceful and private excursion. Fortunately, I found a villager who was willing to guide me using his horses to reach isolated areas. The cost per hour to do this was high so I chose to go for part of the day. We traveled deep into a valley which had many forks from it to other regions. In a brief amount of time I had the privilege of seeing a wide variety of sights and I was thankful for the opportunity to visit places that few tourists go. During the return ride to the city of Gorme, where we had begun, we stopped on top of a ridge to look back at the panorama of rock formations. On a distant ridge I saw a giant triangular shaped erosion that captivated my attention. It was over 100 feet high and had numerous holes in it which looked as if they could be windows. I wanted to see it up close but my guide and I needed to return the horses to the stable. Within a half an hour of riding we arrived back at our destination.

There were still several hours of daylight so I decided to attempt to retrace the way back to get a closer view the large rock projection that seemed so unusual. I knew this was a risky undertaking because of the chance of getting lost in such a labyrinth landscape. Hiking through this area involved taking a series of turns that needed to be memorized for the return trip. Fortunately my sense of direction was good enough to enable me to reach the valley below the rock formation by early evening. From this distance I saw a large carved opening at the base of the cone and I could hear singing coming from inside. This confirmed to me that I had come upon a cave church. I managed to reach the church after a steep climb up a ridge. No one was at the door when I arrived, so I entered part way to see what was happening. There was a group of about twenty Turkish people singing and praying. Candles were flickering from shelves which had been hewn in the rock wall and a cross was visible above the altar before them. Colorfully painted frescos adorned the walls. Suddenly, as I stood there, I became overwhelmed with a sense of a divine presence and my body began to tremble.

I began backing away from the entrance and noted that the people had finished their worship and were preparing to exit.

The first one out of the door was a man who surprised me by speaking English. His first words were, "Are you a Christian?" I said yes even though it was not really true. It seemed as if God was asking me if I was willing yet to profess my faith in Christ. The man told me that the Turkish people worshiping with him were Christians and had traveled several days from Istanbul to worship in this special place. I learned that this cave church had an ancient Christian history and they had chosen that Sunday to visit. I had been oblivious to what day of the week it was.

The congregation exited the church and warmly greeted me as they passed by. When they walked down the hill to the village below I went inside the church to the cross alter. Tears filled my eyes as I prayed and thanked God for revealing His reality to me once more. I asked for the courage to profess my faith in Christ as my Savior and follow His leading in my life. Upon leaving the church the sun was lower in the sky and I knew that within less than two hours it would be totally dark. I quickly hiked back the way I had come and had an uncanny sense of which turns I should make. As the sky became dark I arrived back at the place I was staying. I do not believe that it was simply coincidence or any special skill of mine that allowed me to find the church and return so easily.

CHAPTER 10

CHRISTIAN COMMITMENT AND WORKING FOR MOTHER TERESA

Summer had just begun as I returned from traveling in Turkey. Due to my experience at the cave church in Cappadocia I desired to seek out a place of worship in Seattle. In my childhood I had usually attended church because it was prompted by my parents. Now my motivation to be at a church service was to hear teachings from the Bible and to be in a unique place where I could worship God with others and experience His presence. A large nondenominational Christian church became my spiritual home. I rarely missed a Sunday service because I enjoyed worshiping there so much. Sadly, although I was convinced of the truth of the Christian beliefs, I still was not willing to commit myself as a believer. My stumbling block was the fear of how my life might change if I whole heartedly professed belief in Christ. Many weeks passed as I continued to attend church and glean insights from the pastors messages based on portions of scripture. A strong inner turmoil developed within me because my heart was urging me to make a profession of faith but my will stopped me. Finally, one afternoon I decided to act on my convictions. I prayed a confession of faith in Christ as God. In addition to this I asked for His mercy to forgive my self-centeredness and guide my life. It was reassuring to know that I could trust God to be involved in my life as He had in the past. Even if my future circumstances were difficult I was confident that his purpose for me would be accomplished. No longer would I shrink back from identifying myself as a Christian and telling others about how I came to faith. Within a short time I told my close friends about my change of heart and they expressed a genuine interest in hearing the reasons why I had come to make such a radical turn-around from agnosticism. Prior to mentioning my faith to co-workers, several remarked that they noticed that I seemed more cheerful and wondered why. I also began to receive compliments on how consistently calm I was. This was a confirmation to me that they could see the evidence of my inner peace. The satisfaction this gave me is indescribable.

My zeal for overseas travel persisted but I wanted to do more than just sightsee and have adventure. I desired to give of myself in some way. During past travel in India I had learned some interesting details about Mother Teresa's work in Calcutta and was encouraged to volunteer. At that time I wasn't inclined to be associated with Christian work but now it seemed very appropriate for me to pursue as a new believer. In addition to serving others I could learn how this remarkable woman lived out her faith. Within a few weeks of writing her to express my desire to volunteer I received a letter from her office inviting me to come. Not long after that I was on my way to Calcutta. My plan was to obtain housing in a guest house for missionaries located near the 'Mother House', the convent where Mother Teresa lived with a group of the Catholic Sisters serving in her Missionary of Charity ministry. Reservations were not an option so I had to trust that a room would be available.

The travel from Seattle to Calcutta took more than a day. When I arrived it was evening and I longed for rest. The cab ride from the airport jolted me out of my drowsiness as it sped through the maze of dense street congestion. People and animals randomly crossed the streets as vehicles dodged them. There were no traffic lights, just an occasional circular roundabout at an intersection with a man in uniform directing the traffic. Much to my relief I arrived at the guest house gate without incident. As I was lifting my backpack out of the cab an employee of the guest house approached and told me to leave because there were no vacancies. I then learned that there was a long waiting list to get in and that nothing would be available for several weeks. My heart sunk as I thought of forging my way through the city on foot to find a place to stay. Suddenly a British woman yelled from the guest house veranda for the guard to open the gate because she had a room for me. I was dumbfounded and elated. The cab left and I entered the courtyard to meet her. I found out that she was a long term guest who was working for Mother Teresa. She had overheard my conversation with the guard and decided to intervene to have me stay. Although the place was filled to capacity, she stated that I could stay with her in her small cubicle.

She had squeezed a cot into an alcove next to her bed to store supplies which had been donated for ministry. Her plan was to allow me to sleep on the cot and have the supplies moved elsewhere. It just so happened that my arrival coincided with her recent elimination of over half of her supplies. I was relieved and amazed by this turn of events. My sleep that night was refreshing and in the morning I began to familiarize myself with my surroundings.

The guest house was truly a haven within the noise and squalor of the city. It was a two- level British- style building with room for approximately 50 occupants. Decades earlier it had been used to house men who were in training to be Anglican priests. A lounge, dining area, bathing area and prayer room created a family home ambiance. Only a few cramped, but private, sleeping rooms were available. Generally the guests slept on cots lined up in rows in three large rooms. Each cot was encircled by a mosquito net. Trees and flowers adorned the gardens around the building and there was a giant old stone cathedral on the property. Brick walls secured the perimeter of the property. In striking contrast to the quietness and beauty of this complex was the atmosphere outside the gate. A four- lane city street known as the Lower Circular Road was teeming with people, animals, large diesel trucks, busses, man- pulled rickshaws and cars. Along the sidewalks were people living under tarp shelters. It was heart wrenching to see so many individuals suffering without adequate food or shelter.

One block away from my new' home' was the Mother House, serving as the hub for Mother Teresa's multi faceted ministry. The large multilevel whitewashed building had been purchased for her by the Indian archdiocese a few years after she was given permission to form her own Catholic order to serve the poor. Volunteers for her work were welcome to visit at all hours of the day. My first entry into this historic place was to meet with the Sister who assigned volunteers their jobs.

The 'Mother House' in Calcutta, India

With a bit of anxious anticipation I knocked on the towering door of the Mother House and was greeted by a Sister. Her cheerfulness and warmth calmed my nerves. Inside was a simple large courtyard with cement tile floors and a large shrine of St. Mary as a focal point. The floors above were framed by balconies which were visible from the courtyard. I was ushered upstairs to a small meeting room past a towering life-size crucifix of Christ on the wall with the words in bold letters to the side of it that said, "I thirst".

The mission's sister who met with me was in charge of volunteers for Mother Teresa's mission centers in the Calcutta region. I was aware that there were about ten missions but was most familiar with the work of the orphanage near the Mother House called the *Shishu Bhavan* and the home for the dying which was named *Nirmal Hriday*. Another mission I had very limited knowledge of was the mission for lepers. Working in a leper colony interested me because I wanted to work alongside the medical team as they treated patients.

When the sister asked what type of mission I desired to help with, I responded that I wanted to serve where I was needed the most. I had previously decided not to have a self- serving agenda for my service. She was very appreciative and stated that most of the volunteers' first choice was the orphanage. The place that I was assigned was the home for the mentally ill. I inwardly gasped because I had always felt uncomfortable around the severely mentally ill. When I inquired about the mission for the lepers I was told that there were two. The one in Calcutta did not have volunteers participate and the one in a region north of Calcutta only accepted two volunteers for a month long commitment. Volunteers had already been assigned for the following two months, so I placed myself on a waiting list for the next opening. My meeting with the Sister concluded after I was given more details about the Missionary of Charities ministries and the wide variety of volunteer opportunities. I planned to volunteer for three months and hoped to be able to participate in more than one mission.

As I walked through the courtyard of the Mother House to exit, I caught my first glimpse of Mother Teresa. She was greeting a group of distinguished-appearing visitors. Some in the group were photographers who were taking endless photos. The 'Mother' was gracious and cheerful. I was immediately struck by her small stature and gentle, but commanding presence. What an enormous privilege it was for me to be in the same room with this diminutive and unassuming woman who had become world renown simply because she was willing to fully give of herself to honor God's calling on her life. Through reading her biography I knew that she was absolutely certain that she had received the mandate from God to serve those whom she called the 'poorest of the poor.' She defined herself as God's instrument.

Within a week of arrival in Calcutta I was spending most of my days at the mission for the mentally ill, known as *Prem Dan*. It was located adjacent to railroad tracks near a slum area. The building was a large two level cement structure with very few windows. On the lower level were over- size rooms, each to accommodate approximately one hundred sleeping cots. The facility housed up to 300 patients. There was an open- air bathing area to the back and a patio near the front entrance.

The severity of mental illness that many of the occupants had was more pronounced than I had ever seen. Some maintained a continuous catatonic squatting position and didn't speak. My job was to assist the mission's Sisters and other volunteers with the full care of these patients. Each morning they were bathed and given clean clothes. This was an arduous chore because many needed to be carried to a communal bathing area where each were hand-bathed before being taken to the dressing area. After each patient was dressed they were carried or assisted to the patio area to sit outside and have food. Workers divided up their duties so that some would stay outside with the patients and help them eat while the others worked inside to clean the sleeping rooms and the dirty clothes.

The cleaning process was shockingly primitive. Water was heated over gas flames prior to being poured into large pots which held the dirty clothes. All the clothes were washed by hand and then hung on lines to dry in the sun. The sleeping rooms required cot and floor scrubbing every day because so many patients were incontinent during the night. This process required removing the soiled sheets, wiping down each waterproof cot with disinfectant, stacking all of the cots to the side of the room and then scrubbing the cement floor. After the floor was scrubbed it was hosed down and the water swept off into drainage areas. The chores were more labor- intensive than I had ever experienced. Each afternoon I would return to my guest house and collapse with fatigue. The emotional toll of the work was greater than the physical effects. Seeing the degree of misery all around me resulted in a profound inner distress. I wrestled with why God would allow such suffering. Each day as I walked to *Prem Dan* I passed people living in inhumane conditions alongside the streets. This, in addition to seeing the condition of the mentally ill, caused me deep sadness. I realized if I continued in this emotional state I could not work effectively and would need to leave Calcutta.

One night while lying awake on my cot I decided to get up and go to the chapel room of the guest house to pray. I did not want to abandon the work

I had begun and I desperately needed to have God intervene. I prayed that God would help me understand His ways and give me peace. In addition to prayer, I decided to read my personal travel Bible because I knew that God speaks through His written word. At random I opened to a passage of scripture. As I read I pondered the words and then prayed. My text had cross references which gave information about where certain themes or words were used in other chapters or books of the Bible. I intently read the portions of scripture which were noted. A key theme that ended up being the focus was God's mercy and goodness, coupled with the fact that "His ways are not our ways."(Isaiah 55:8) I began to understand that there will be things He allows that I will not be able to understand. I knew then that I must trust in His love for mankind and accept that it is not for me to question his ways.

My time in the chapel seemed brief but it became apparent that I had been there several hours when I heard the bells ring from the nearby cathedral announcing early morning worship. Many people began filing into the cathedral but I did not plan to attend. It usually was part of my routine, but I reasoned that I had already had my worship, and that if I went back to bed I could get two hours of sleep before a long day.

Immediately after this thought entered my mind, I was overwhelmed with the memory of a Bible verse in Psalm 122:1 which says," I rejoiced with those who said to me let us go to the house of the Lord." When I considered what a privilege it is to gather with others and worship, I decided to go.

Hurriedly, I changed out of my night-wear and went to the cathedral. I was the last one to enter, so I tried to be as inconspicuous as possible. As I sat down on the pew I heard the priest say, "I was glad when they said let us go into the house of the Lord." That seemed to be an amazing coincidence. After a time of prayer the priest asked me if I would read the epistle for the day. The epistles provided for the service were compilations of scripture that addressed a certain theme. I opened to the days reading and as I began to read I could feel my heart pounding. The scriptures for the day were the very ones I had been reading through the night! I then knew that God was reemphasizing to me what He wanted me to know.

What had occurred was something I do not feel could be explained away as simply serendipity or coincidence. My prayer for peace of mind had been answered and I knew my work in India could continue.

The weeks passed by as I gradually adjusted to the work demands and developed friendships with others in the guest house. One of the guests was volunteering as a teacher at a Missionary of Charities school for street children. He asked if I would be willing to take his place when he left. I learned that he had obtained permission to appoint a replacement from the Sister in charge of the volunteers. This request was timely for me. I needed a change from the hard labor at *Prem Dan* because of the toll it was taking on my body. I committed to taking on the new job despite limited teaching experience. My uneasiness about the teaching role was quelled by the knowledge that the Sisters at the school would help me and that I could trust God to give me wisdom.

The school was located near a slum that bordered a garbage dump. People in the slums eked out an existence from what they retrieved from the garbage piles.

Street dwellers near garbage dump

The children of the slums had no means to obtain an education and without it were likely to continue the slum lifestyle as adults. Mother Teresa's school provided a daily bath, clean clothes, food and education. Every afternoon when schooling ended the youngsters were placed back in their freshly laundered street clothes to return to family. This was the practice for two reasons. Firstly, each child needed clean clothes each day after their bath and secondly, if the children left wearing nice clothes the tendency was for the families to sell them for money.

The first day at the Gandhi School I knew that my job would be joyful. All of the workers were cheerful and enthusiastic, and the children were loving and exuberant. It was truly a blessing to be in such an uplifting atmosphere. The Sister in charge of the school had joined Mother Teresa several decades earlier. She exuded a love and gentleness that I admired.

By the time I arrived every day, the children had finished their bath and breakfast. The classes would begin promptly and last for several hours. Each class had approximately ten students who had already learned English. My role was to teach them math and reading. They were all very eager to please when doing their assignments because they craved love. At first I felt overwhelmed by children all wanting my attention at the same time, but I soon learned ways to structure the teaching to enable me to give undivided time to each one. The afternoon schedule was full of non classroom interaction. A hearty lunch was served and then playtime followed. Numerous games were led by the workers. It was such a delight to see the children having so much fun because I knew their lives were so hard. The school day ended with a time of singing and prayer. It was sad to think of the little ones leaving the school each day to live in desperate conditions but I was consoled with the knowledge that they would be in a community with family.

One month after working with the children, I was notified that I had been chosen to assist at a leper colony. Saying good-bye at the school was unbelievably difficult. Going to the leper colony also meant leaving the guest house and becoming a resident worker at a mission located several hundred miles north of the city.

I departed Calcutta by train with a fellow volunteer to spend the following month in a place that few people see. The train arrived in the town of Chitarajhan after five hours.

The leper colony, known as *Shanti Nagar*, was located several miles from the train station. A bicycle rickshaw provided transport through the arid countryside to access our destination. Along the way we passed many mud brick homes with tile roofs. The front yards of these very simple abodes were usually swept dirt with chalk artwork. Most dwellings had cow dung plastered to the outside walls to dry in the sun in preparation for use as fire fuel. The dirt road on which we traveled was frequented by locals transporting loads by ox- pulled carts. The entire scene caused me to feel as though I had stepped back in time.

Shanti Nagar (meaning 'village of peace') was an unexpectedly beautiful place. It was a walled- in community occupying several acres which included trees, gardens and farmland. Many lepers lived there with their families. The place was quite self- sufficient. Pigs and chickens were farmed for meat and vegetable gardens provided produce. Grain was provided through donations to the mission and then made into the traditional flat bread called *chapatti*. There were homes for the families, housing for the workers, a church, school, bakery, pharmacy, custom shoe making facility and a graveyard.

I had expected to encounter a lot of sadness inside the leper colony. Much to my amazement the people were cheerful and outgoing. Many had disfigurement from the disease but interacted with others as if they had no disability. It became apparent that they were very appreciative of their circumstances despite having a disease. Within a day I was feeling very much a part of the group. Accommodations for my co-volunteer and me, was in a building adjacent to the Jesuit priest's quarters. Our meals would be eaten with him in his private dining area because of the lack of room elsewhere. The priest was an elderly man from Belgium whom I warmed to instantly. He was kind, gentle, well spoken and an interesting conversationalist.

Mother Teresa had developed the *Shanti Nagar* mission to help the lepers emotionally as well as physically. I was informed that she did not view their illness as the biggest problem. Her belief was that the overriding issue was their sense of being unloved and unwanted in society. She envisioned a place where lepers could live in community with family and maintain self respect by being allowed to build their own homes and work their own fields. Within this community they could also have the medical and spiritual support they needed. Leprosy (medically termed Hansen's disease) was once believed to be highly contagious but that has since been proven wrong. Despite this, the affliction continues to have a negative social stigma and those with the disease tend to be shunned from society. I had never known much about leprosy and had never seen the disfiguring skin lesions it causes. As I assisted with wound care, I learned that the disease affects the nerves, especially in the arms and legs. If the disease progresses, the limbs become weak, lose peripheral sensation, and often become deformed or have tissue loss. Some patients were missing limbs because of not getting treatment in a timely manner. Being able to interact and contribute to the care of these people was deeply gratifying to me.

For one month I was privileged to be a part of this special community. The workers and residents were one big family. I had come to serve but found that I was often the one being served. The women in the bakery taught me how to make chapattis. The pharmacist taught me about the drugs and the dispensing system, the shoe makers showed me their skills in creating custom shoes, the farming techniques were shared and the children entertained me with songs and games. I was invited to enjoy worship services and the priest shared many interesting books from his library. St Francis of Assisi was so insightful when he stated, *"For it is in giving that we receive."* The weeks passed by at a rapid pace and I wished I could have stayed longer. Memories from there still bring a smile to my face.

Prior to leaving India I spent an additional week in Calcutta. During this time I seized the opportunity to frequent the Mother House. The visits were primarily to attend morning mass with Mother Teresa and the Sisters. Each person sat on a mat on the floor. I would sit near the back and often Mother Teresa would be across the aisle from me. I still envision her weathered hands folded in prayer and think about how much she had used those hands to extend a compassionate touch to someone in need. Something that deeply stirred my soul during the mass was listening to the Sisters singing a cappella. The sound was angelic.

Sisters at worship in Mother House

A special event occurred just a couple days before my departure. Mother Teresa called a private meeting with a few of the volunteers working locally. Her desire was to encourage and thank each one. We all sat around her on the floor as she spoke with us and asked for feedback about our experience. She was an active listener which I felt gave an indication of how much she honored others.

At the end of the time together she gave each one in the room a pendant. An added special blessing to me was having her write 'God bless you' in my travel Bible. When she finished she looked up at me and said, "Always remember to pray."

Mother Teresa giving pendants to the volunteers

My conclusion as to why Mother Teresa was so successful was that she had a sincere devotion to Jesus Christ as the Lord of her life and she diligently sought his leading through prayer many times a day. She had convictions that were unwavering, even when she was harshly criticized. Her fulfillment was in doing God's will instead of getting accolades from others. It is my desire to always emulate her dependence on God, her compassion, selflessness and perseverance in doing what God had placed on her heart.

CHAPTER 11

ANSWERED PRAYER

The perspective I had on life after returning from Calcutta was very different from what it had been prior to leaving. Material possessions and fun activities seemed trivial compared to impacting others lives in a meaningful way. My yearning was to continue to experience God through prayer and Bible study and use my abilities to honor Him. I had no grand plan except to be loving toward others in a selfless way. Two statements which were imbedded in my mind were: "You can do no great things but you can do small things with great love." (Mother Teresa) and "In his heart man plans his ways but the Lord determines his steps." (NIV Bible, Proverbs 16:9)

I had a heart to serve in overseas missions and felt I would be well-suited for that lifestyle because of previous experiences. In order to have the flexibility to leave at a moment's notice I refrained from renting an apartment and instead purchased an Airstream trailer from my parents and lived in it on their property. My hospital work resumed as a nurse in the ICU. Within a few months I had connected well in a neighborhood church and agreed to help with the youth ministry. What I discovered was that I thoroughly enjoyed interacting with the young people of varying ages and that my work with the children in Calcutta had been excellent preparation. I kept thinking that eventually mission work would captivate my attention, but I was mistaken. The longer I worked as a youth leader, the less I desired to leave. I realized that my heart was not for overseas missions in the near future and that my place of service was in Seattle. I stayed living in my trailer and doing youth work for several years.

The time came when I knew it was time to move from my cramped living space. I also wanted to begin making an investment in a home. My criteria for a home was that it would be within the general area that my parents lived so that I could be available to help them as they got older. Additionally, I did not want a place that would burden me financially, and I desired pleasant surroundings.

I prayed diligently for God's help in finding the right place. Soon I discovered that small homes were far beyond my budget. When I investigated some of the condominiums nearby I found that the prices were equally as high. Most of the places did not even meet my criteria due to being located on busy streets. I was discouraged and resigned to finding a rental until I could save more money. Oddly enough, before I began looking for a rental, a mission opportunity presented itself. I was asked to be one of the leaders for a group of Christian teens doing a service project in a poor community in Peru. I readily agreed and began preparations.

One week prior to leaving, something very unexpected occurred. A close friend of mine from my church announced that she and her husband had a condominium that they needed to sell. It had been co-owned by her husband and his father. His father had lived there for many years but suddenly decided to move out. They were getting ready to bid on a new home and needed cash soon. I was offered a private showing prior to them placing it on the market. Even though I had informed them of my limited funds they encouraged me to take a look. They desired to refrain from discussing the price until after I had seen it. Viewing the condo took my breath away. I loved its design and location. I was prepared for a big letdown when I asked the price. At their response I asked them to repeat themselves because I thought I had heard incorrectly. Unbelievably, they were asking nearly half of what I expected. Without hesitation I committed to a purchase. My transition to home ownership couldn't have been better. Prior to leaving for Peru I was able to get the proper paperwork in order for the purchase and then move in immediately after returning from the mission trip.

My new place suited me perfectly. In addition to being affordable and in a good location, it had extra features I had always dreamed of having in a home: a sunken living room with vaulted ceilings, a fireplace and a large space for a library and study. One drawback was that there was not enough storage space. A solution for this came when I was able to purchase a garage from an elderly couple in the building.

I am grateful for a peaceful place to live but even more grateful for my inner peace. My relationship with God is the source of my peace. In the not too distant past, I have had to deal with an infection which resulted in hospitalization for ten days and then shortly after that the death of my father. Although I was dealing with so much distress, I can honestly say I had the abiding peace of God. He is more real to me than anything visible. I am convinced that I have been blessed so that I can bless others. He has revealed his reality to me so that I can give an account to others. As I look to the future I am confident that my life's purpose will be fulfilled. I encourage you to watch for 'God sightings' and seek to know Him. The Bible says in James 4:8, "Come near to God and he will come near to you." My heartfelt closing words are from Romans 15:13a, "May the God of hope fill you with all joy and peace as you trust in him."

EPILOGUE

I would encourage you to objectively examine your faith. Even if you don't view yourself as a faith person, you do have faith because even atheists have faith that their viewpoint is the most reasonable. Is what you believe worthy of the faith you place in it? Have you thought out why you believe what you do? Your beliefs affect every aspect of your life, especially your inner peace. If the Bible is God's word to man, as it claims to be, there are eternal consequences to rejecting God's revealed truth.

When I was soul searching and seeking to determine what I believed was worthy of my faith, I wish the book <u>Choosing Your Faith (<i>In A World of Spiritual Options</i>)</u> by Mark Mittelberg had been available. It gives information about the varying belief systems and how to choose wisely. I highly recommend the book and urge you to read it.